Journey to Enlightenment

Juliet Christie Murray

(Soy Criada)

Note for Librarians: a cataloguing record for this book that includes Dewey
Decimal Classification and US Library of Congress numbers is available
from the National Library of Canada. The complete cataloguing record can
be obtained from the National Library's online database at:
www.nlc-bnc.ca/amicus/index-e.html
ISBN 1-4120-3623-2

Printed in Victoria, BC, Canada.

TRAFFORD

Offices in Canada, USA, Ireland, UK and Spain
This book was published on-demand in cooperation with Trafford
Publishing. On-demand publishing is a unique process and service of
making a book available for retail sale to the public taking advantage of
on-demand manufacturing and Internet marketing. On-demand publishing
includes promotions, retail sales, manufacturing, order fulfilment,
accounting and collecting royalties on behalf of the author.
Book sales for North America and international:
Trafford Publishing, 6E-2333 Government St.,
Victoria, BC V8T 4P4 CANADA
phone 250 383 6864 (toll-free 1 888 232 4444)
fax 250 383 6804; email to orders@trafford.com
Book sales in Europe:
Trafford Publishing (UK) Ltd., Enterprise House, Wistaston Road Business
Centre, Wistaston Road, Crewe, Cheshire CW2 7RP
UNITED KINGDOM
phone 01270 251 396 (local rate 0845 230 9601)
facsimile 01270 254 983; orders.uk@trafford.com

www.trafford.com/robots/04-1451.html

10 9 8 7 6 5

Life has its many problems and sometimes they seem to overpower us. Here is a book that will help you over the difficult times and help to smooth the rough patches. It will help you to pick up the pieces and move on.

A book of encouragement written from an angle you may not have seen before.

JOURNEY TO ENLIGHTENMENT is an anthology of poems that deal with social, spiritual, political and emotional issues and spans a wide cross section of cultures. The poems are current and are appropriate to the times.

Dedicated to

My husband Reuben who has put up with my many shortcomings when I was writing this book.

My son Dwight who encouraged me when I had second thoughts about writing this book.

My son Garth for understanding me.

My grand daughter Sabrina who loves me so much.

I love you all.

Acknowledgement

I want to express my gratitude to Mrs. Vilma Kameka for encouraging me on the path to writing this anthology, without her I would not have known that I had the ability to put all these thoughts on paper. Vilma more power to you.

To Miss Eugenie Simpson who helped me in arranging some of the lines that were very difficult. To Mrs. Anita J. Small-Murray; Mrs. Marva Trenfield who helped with the editing and Mr. Hopeton Grey who gave me much valid information and encouragement. To all the individuals who gave me inspirations, students at the Sandy Bay Primary and Junior High school where I work; and individuals with their various life experiences.

Many thanks.

Table of Contents

Introduction

'Journey To Enlightenment' is written surrounding observations and experiences both of the author and other individuals. In this book there are thoughts of encouragement to people who may have lost the drive and the zeal to face some of life's most challenging situations. This is what this book is all about, to encourage the human spirit.

It aims to show individuals that life is made up of many choices and each individual should know what is desired in life and make the right choice. The right choice, eventually makes you and your spirit feel comfortable when you have made it. This book was written as if it was directed by an invisible force, as seen in the last piece 'Revelation'.

I surprised even myself by writing this book. I was unaware that I had the talent for this. It covers a wide cross section of society in topics such as politics as in 'No Easy Choice,' Love as in 'Love Funny Ways' Inequality, as in; 'Release the Shackles of inequality', the state of the soul, as in 'The Better Part'. This anthology would not be Complete without the inclusion of nature as in the pieces 'Rain Dance', 'Debil an Him Wife' and 'Farewell'.

'Journey To Enlightenment' is written based on a sociological background of observations and opinions It is hoped that persons who read these poems find some words that encourage and give them enthusiasm and strength to buoy the spirit along life's journey.

Happy reading.

Journey To Enlightenment

I am buried in this dark hot mucky ship's hull,
At the bottom of this ship
Is where my journey will begin,
But I will survive this journey,
I will rise from this ship's hull
Though my journey has just begun.

From Africa's coast I come,
The Caribbean will be my new home.
Although throughout this journey
I will be bound by shackles of
Iron, chain and clamps,
When my journey is ended
I will be free.

My Capturers think they are my masters,
They think I am a stupid fool
And will try to use me as a tool,
Men will bid for me and even cast lots for me,
But one day when my journey is ended,
I and my mind will be free.

Yes I have no fear for this trip,
For soon I will be free from
This dark, hot, mucky hull of this illiteracy ship,
Up I will come through the passages of enlightenment
To stand proud on a platform of literacy,
No longer will I be a passenger of this ship,
For, I too will become a master.
Freedom, Freedom, Freedom!

Journey to Enlightenment

Will be mine.

February 18, 2004.Black history month: remembering the journey of slaves from Africa to the West Indies. It is likened to been enslaved in the ignorance of illiteracy.

Juliet Christie Murray

Caribbean Laments

Great, big U.S.A,
What have you done
To my children?
You courted them
With opportunities,
You offered them
Wealth,
Technology,
Jobs,
And a better way of life,
"The sky is the limit "you told them,
"I am the land of opportunities,"
You said, so you took them in.

You took my best,
My brightest,
My most ambitious,
You offered them
What they believed
I could not give,
You took my athletes,
My scholars and my professionals,
Yet you forsook them in their times
Of most distress and greatest need.

You work them,
You spurn them,
You covet them
For their ambition,
You took what they

Had to offer,
And gave very little in return,
You were so surprised to find
Embedded in these my people
So much, to make you great.

In return you gave them trophies to hang
On the walls of your basements,
Amidst the squalor of poverty and hunger.
You have caused many of them to suffer,
To become wanderers,
Living aimlessly on your streets
And beneath your bridges,
Hiding from the scorching sun
And the biting snow,
Without love, without family, without home,
Shattered hopes,
As these my most ambitious sons,
Will never see my face again.

They have lost their zeal,
Their desire for a better tomorrow.
They have become destitute,
And pray they could return,
To my loving arms again,
But free ride
Is not your style for free men?
Only for criminals and murderers,
I know I could love them better,
Or even the same,
Great, Big! U.S.A.
What have you done
To my Children?

Juliet Christie Murray

August 2002. Written after visiting Brooklyn New York and saw how a number of West Indian Blacks Live.

The U. S.A. now Deports West Indians who have broken Her laws. Some of these individuals lived in the U.S.A. since they were children.

Love Funny Ways

I love you, he said,
For your sweet smile
And pleasant ways
Your sweet love
And your tenderness.
You are like fresh dew
From heaven above
You'll be the centre
Of my whole world
So, I'll love you,

Until

The sun ceases to shine
Till the flowers have
Lost their smell,
Till the days get colder
If you just walk
This way with me.
So he became
My joy,
And my life,
As we shared all I ever had.

Myself.
My time
My love
My affection
My emotions and
My wealth.

Juliet Christie Murray

He took all I ever owned,
I gave and he took,
But one thing I'm now sure
He never ever lied.

He gave,
Just what he said
He had to give.
Just when he started
Loving me until my
Sun stopped shining,
I cannot really tell,
For I was just too busy,
Colouring and perfuming
His world.

But now my eyes are opened.
And I am quite certain,
I'll never let him,
Ever,
Cause me to lose
My perfume,
Or let my days
Get colder,
And go way down
Below zero.

Nov 28, 2002. Written the day after speaking to a woman who was experiencing emotional problems with her husband.

Is It The Name

It's now lunchtime,
This child said he would sing
If he got twenty dollars
He got it,
So he sang,
That's how he is
Strong
Proud
Never looking for hand outs,
This half cast son
Of a black Jamaican father
And a white European mother.

He was given the name Caleb,
Now only twelve years old
And cannot read,
But is determined
That he is going to read,
And will not join his mother
In her homeland,
Until he is able to shake off
This yoke of illiteracy
Within his father's land.

But his load is huge
And very heavy,
For survival is his game
As he carries the weight
Of his own future,
The past mistakes of his mother

Juliet Christie Murray

And his father thrown together
In cultures alien to both,
Cultures they did not understand
Where love mushroomed into hatred.

He shapes his own destiny,
A true product of the saying
You are your own destiny.
To survive he rears chickens,
He does his own fishing
Sleeps wherever it's convenient,
Yet deep within him burns the fire
That makes men truly free,
The ability to read.

Four years he spent
In a reading class,
But the survival instinct
To that path he went,
Caleb, a man of courage
Will always see very far
And so,
Surveying the distant future
One day he said,
"Teacher it's time I leave this class."

"But Caleb", said the teacher,
"Sure you will not survive out there,
Because for grade seven
You are surely not prepared."
"Let's strike a bargain then", she said,
"Reading class in the mornings,
Grade seven in the evenings",
"A bargain then it is dear teach",

Journey to Enlightenment

"Then, let us sign a contract now",
The teacher said.
And so the contract they both signed.
And as a strong, true Caleb
He kept his part of the bargain.
This man, living
Within the body of a child.

Oct. 18,2002. The fight of a student against illiteracy; a teacher's flexibility;
The appreciation for the competency shelter programme in Jamaican schools,
especially for the Sandy Bay Primary and Junior High School; A salute to all
competency shelter teachers.

Juliet Christie Murray

Keeping My Cool

This morning I'm feeling glorious,
Ready to impart to
These youthful minds,
Ready to change the way they think
And give meaning
To their young lives,
I guess that's pretty cool.

Few hours later
I'm feeling less glorious
Less energized,
As the noise of indiscipline
Escalates in octaves
Overcasting my sunshine
With its great crescendo,
But I'm still feeling pretty cool.

Then entered a visitor
"Good day madam",
"How are you?
I am here to video your school,
The block
That my colleague donated
To these lovely students of yours".
I am now trying
To hang on to my cool.

I looked up and saw
Bags of water go
Sailing through the air,

Journey to Enlightenment

Wetting students, teachers, visitors and all,
I wondered was that on video too
Has our school gone international
With indiscipline?
Tell me, isn't it now time
I give in, and lose my cool?

Written Thursday June 27 2002 at school after receiving a visitor from the U.S.A.

Juliet Christie Murray

Live Coals Of Love

They met as strangers,
"Hi" he said, " you seem to have money
Could you take me to the show"?
"Sure", said she,
"Why not"?

This started a gentle flame
That burst into a fire,
That ignited two twigs
One bounded to a tree
The other surely free.

This fire kept on burning,
Though one was not bold enough
To pluck the other from its tree,
Fearing the other could not survive,
Not bounded to its tree.

And so the ashes settled
Over these two live coals,
A decade past and the one free
Wanting its own tree, soared away
To be bounded to it's own tree.

It took only a birthday card,
Exchanged over the next decade
To say the flames though burn low
Had not completely died,
Although each is now
Bounded to its own tree.

Journey to Enlightenment

However,
The sky, the ocean,
A continent, a new land,
A mighty rushing
Wind of wings.

Was enough to
Ignite a flame in
These two live coals
More powerful than
Two decades ago.

Will these coals
Be bold enough
Be strong enough
Be hot enough
To burn each its own tree?

Or will they allow
Ashes to settle,
As they did
Two decades ago.

August 2002 .New York City, U.S.A., a love story of two people who love each other but have previous commitment to other individuals.

Juliet Christie Murray

Look At Them

Look at them
Standing, sitting there,
The present, the past, the future!
All wrapped up in these bundles
Of humanity waiting to emerge.

They are hoping that some one will notice,
Will give much attention!
Will give precedence
To these bundles
Of humanity bursting to emerge.

For in them we see ourselves
Of what we have become,
Would become, and hope
That they perpetuate us, these
Bundles of humanity hoping to emerge.

They hold the future of our country,
They will some day
Control the world,
These, whom we have given,
The best we could afford.

And today we look on,
Proud to know we have played
Our part in helping
These bundles of humanity,
Joyfully and triumphantly emerge.

Journey to Enlightenment

Written June 10.2002.Sitting at my teaching desk observing a class of students sitting before me.

The last two verses were added after attending my last son's graduation for his Bachelors degree in Architecture. Nov 2, 2002, at 23 years old.

Dedicated to all the teachers who have taught my son Dwight Antonio Murray.

Juliet Christie Murray

No Easy Choice

(Jamaican dialect)

A black man time now!
We all seh a black people time
Fi form Government
And have wi own black prime minister
Fi gi wi equal rights and justice.

A oofa time it really be though?
We talk bout globalization
A who really deh globalize who?
A black man a globalize white man,
Or a white man a globalize all?

We seh a black man time now,
For we want equality and justice,
An a Syrian man can' never gi
Black man equal rights and justice,
So it fall pan the black man fi do it.

You believe black man can gi
Equality and justice when him neva
Get a chance fi know the meaning,
Much less fi have it fi gi it weh
In a dem ya hard time yah?

You no see seh white man a use inequality
And injustice fi globalize the whole worl?
And as far as me caan see, them throw it pan
The poor black Prime Minister dem,

Journey to Enlightenment

And dem in turn, must fling it back pan we.

Written at school Monday Sept. 2002. As the reality of cost sharing hit schools, teachers are faced with problems of trying to make the meager grants work, parents are having hard times in meeting the school fees; election is in the air; Jamaicans are faced with the dilemma of which party to choose to form the next government.

Juliet Christie Murray

No Easy Choice

(English version)

We all say now is Black man's time,
It's black people's time
To form our own government.
Because we want our own
Black prime minister who will give us
Equal rights and justice.

Whose time really, is it?
We talk about globalization,
Who really is globalizing the other?
Is it black man globalizing the white man?
Or is it the white man globalizing all?

We say its black man's time now!
For we want equality and justice,
And a Syrian man can never give
Black man equal rights and justice,
So it falls to the black man to do this.

Do you believe black man can give
Equality and justice,
When he has never ever gotten
The chance to know the meaning,
More so to have it to give it away
Especially in these hard times?

Do you not see that the white man
Is using inequality and injustice

To globalize the whole world
And as far as can be seen,
It is passed unto the poor
Third world black prime ministers,
Who in turn must pass it on to us.

Written at school Monday Sept.2002. As the reality of cost sharing hit schools, teachers are faced with problems of trying to make the meager grants work; parents are having hard times in meeting the school fees; election is in the air; Jamaicans are faced with the dilemma of which party to choose to form the next government.

Juliet Christie Murray

Who Are You

Who you are is what
You make your self to be.
Would you be one of the small lights?
Narrow in intellect
And mentally weak?
Or do you allow
That universal spirit
From which all good deeds leak,
To guide and direct your path?

Do you let wealth purchase your position?
Instead of achieving your profession,
Through hard work and integrity?
Do you elevate yourself above
Human weaknesses and infirmities?
To the point that you care not,
How, what, or whom you compromise,
For the sake of popularity?
Be the guardian of your own integrity.

Swerve not from the better knowledge
Of good, and paralyze prosperity,
Exhibit these qualities of the mind,
Perseverance
Patience
Forbearance
Calm
Courage
Love,
Because in times of crisis there you'll find,

Journey to Enlightenment

Great men of courage are born.

Feb 15. 2003. After listening to some stories of how various individuals used dedication, hard work, courage and integrity to overcome the odds that were against them and so achieved their dreams.

Juliet Christie Murray

Pass It On

Have you ever
Stopped to think on
This vast universe
That surrounds you?
Have you
Considered
The majestic power
Of he who created it?

Do you realize
This was created
Just for you,
Just for me?
You give birth
To a child and think
Of it as one of life's
Greatest miracles.

You seek to give it
All the good things
That is within you,
You embrace it
And you love it.
Have you ever
Stopped to think
You are the child
Of a powerful being?

A being that has
Similar feelings for you?

Journey to Enlightenment

And this is why
He has created
This universe.
Just for you to choose
Whatever you wish from it?
What have you chosen?
Do you wish
To choose all of it?
For this you know,
You'll never be able to do,
Do you therefore choose the best of it?
Knowing that you will
Expand it multiply it
So that you alone cannot contain it?

Or do you choose the worst of it?
Expand on it, multiply on it, and
Pass it on to your children,
Your brother, your sister,
Ignoring the fact
That they too like you
Are capable of doing the same,
Pass it on.

Sitting at my work desk. June 4, 2002. Observing the students and wondering how many of us do realize that most of the values and attitudes seen in people today were passed on to them as children by their parents or guardians.

Juliet Christie Murray

Release the Shackles of Inequality

Rise up you marginalized
Be it by colour, race, or creed,
Be it by gender, wealth,
Position or class,
Rise up! Fight
This inequality.

Go claim what is yours,
Your destiny,
Though it should lie within your hands,
Is still not yours to seize
By yourself alone,
For unity is strength.

Go fight for justice, for
Your share of the wealth,
And do not let capitalistic
Imagery and intention,
Overshadow your quest for your true destiny.

For you are not
Created inferior,
Blind and unintelligent,
But was created a being,
Among all men equal, a superior being.
In the image of your divine creator.

Fight poverty and disease,
Imperialism
Capitalism

Journey to Enlightenment

And racism,
Fight against hunger,
Gender inequality and suppression.

Walk with your head held high,
Be proud
Of whom you are!
An individual
Worthy enough,
An entity of much affluence.
Of whom powerful
Men and nations
Covet, enough to dominate,
Rob and suppress,
Rise up! Shake off
Your shackles of inequality.

You must educate and unite,
For the cause of your despised brother,
Your despised and spurned sister,
Your young generation,
Get back what is truly yours,
For you were born to be free.

August 16, 2002. Recalling social inequality class at Eastern Ct. State University summer 2002.

Juliet Christie Murray

Seize life

Seize life when you can
For time waits for no one,
On the day we are born
We set in motion a clock,
That keeps on working
And never stops,
Until our hearts dictate,
That time for it is done.

So often we accede,
For this clock to tick away.
So many wasted minutes
And opportunities we
Allowed to pass, for,
We say we are invincible,
There is enough time
For youth and health are ours.

So many friends we have met
And lost along the way,
We did not keep in touch,
For we believe they are
Only,
Months
Weeks
Days
Hours, Or
Only miles away,
Only to find that
When we need them most,

Journey to Enlightenment

They are no longer there.

And what about love?
Have we really and truly loved?
Or were the dictates of needs
Or wants allowed to
Quench that fire we felt
For the ones we loved so dear?
Or, did we choose love
Whatever was the cost?

How is our stand on hope?
For a future bright and fair,
For with hope all is possible,
Along with faith so dear,
For hope is what fuel great men,
Of courage and renown,
It's hope that makes us,
Seize life, right now and today.

September 2,2002, looking back in retrospect and thinking of the many things
I would have liked to do but now only to find that because of circumstances I
will not be able to do most. However there is still hope for doing some if the
opportunity of 'now' is utilized.

Juliet Christie Murray

Sitting Here

And I sit here knowing that
These are hard times,
These are the times designed
To bring out the steel in me.

What about your steel?
The inner man,
Will these times
Bend and break your steel?

Or will these hard times
Straighten it as an arrow?
Sending your steel to the
Heights beyond.

Where,
No man can touch it.
Only the almighty can direct it,
To love, to give of self.
Knowing that your steel
Will strengthen the steel
Of your brother,
The steel of your sister
As they entwine
In strength and unity.

June 16, 2002. This is my first piece. I was just sitting and thinking about the hard economic times Jamaica is experiencing and how Jamaicans have to be cooperative and strong to live through the challenging times ahead.

Journey to Enlightenment

Battle of Spirits

"Where he leads me
I will follow,"
Was what he said.
Some said, he is crazy
Others said, he is,
Receiving a call from God.

He heard only these commands,
Go out and heal the world
And no charge,
Wear white,
Drink milk and honey.

Do you know who you are?
Said one wise one.
Read Jeremiah one, that!
Will tell you who you are,
For after fifty a powerful gift
You shall surely receive.

All this I will give thee,
If you will worship me
Was what Satan said
To our Lord Jesus Christ,
What then could he
Not have said to a lowly
Human being like he?

He said I will let you read the
Cards,

Juliet Christie Murray

Candles,
Palms,
Crystal,
Fates,
Lives,
Writings,
I will make you one of the
Most powerful!
Human being on earth.

But only he who knows the
Great almighty,
The most powerful
'I am', that 'I am',
Can discern between
The giver of all the
Gifts and all the calls.

Only he of a meek and
Humble spirit,
Can choose the path
My friend has chosen.
For if he chooses to wear
His white robes and garment,
Symbols of purity of spirit
And righteousness of heart.

Decides to drink milk and honey
The symbols for studying,
God's Holy word,
Make use of the gifts of
Speaking, reading, and writing,
Of inspirational thoughts,
Use the gift of touch

Journey to Enlightenment

To touch some sick and ailing
Sister, in her journey
Along life's road.

What better gifts could he,
Had chosen or be given,
In his quest in helping
His poor,
Lost and ailing brother,
As he struggles along
Life's rugged road?

November 29.2002. A spiritual experience, April 1987; This individual has gone on to study alternate medicines. Give counseling on diet and at age 51 began writing poems of encouragement.

Juliet Christie Murray

The Better Part

I visited a funeral service today
And noticed that there were
The deceased's date of birth,
A dash,
And the deceased's date of death
Beautifully inscribed on the programme.
What does the dash represents?
Our life's journey
The eulogist explained,
The preacher was a woman
Pretty, and rather young.

I wondered why such a
Vibrant, beautiful, young lady
Decided to become a minister.
As I sat and listened
I started to understand.
She took her text
From St. Luke 10,
The story of Mary and Martha,
Mary, the master said,
Had chosen the better part.
What have we included in our dash?

Education
Wealth
Love
Children
Friends?
All those things that have

Journey to Enlightenment

Kept us really busy
Throughout the years,
Or have we like Mary
Chosen the better part?

After the business is over
The children all grown and gone,
The wealth we have all stockpiled,
The lovers we have kept or left,
What next?
Oh yes
We have
Satisfied our hearts deepest desires!
All these we have
Included in our dash,
But have we included the better part?

The part Jesus said Mary had chosen
The part, he said
No one can take away?
What makes up this better part?
This better part comes with much
Sacrifice,
Sacrifice of some of the things
We valued and desired most.
People whom we love
And whose love we gave up
To the point that it broke our hearts.

Yes, this better part sometimes comes
With much sorrow, grief and pain,
But, what a joy and a delight it will be,
When we have finished our dash
And have known that whatever the cost

Juliet Christie Murray

We have finished our dash in dignity,
Because our dash had included
That better part.

Why has this been the better part?
Because, if this life was all we have,
We would be most miserable,
But, we have that hope of the joy
Of that glorious resurrection morn,
When we'll be proud,
To have included Jesus
In our dash.

Written November 2002, after visiting a funeral service of a friend's aunt and was very impressed by the sermon of the young female Methodist Minister.

Journey to Enlightenment

Why Me

You sometime ask the question
Why me?
Of all the persons
Why me?
I who enjoy life
And all its pleasures
Why me?

In the stillness of the night,
In this midnight of your life,
You shed
Bitter tears,
And you continue
To ask the question
Why me God?

Just take time out
To listen,
And you will hear him say,
It was just too late to recall
That destroying angel,
So I did the best I could
For you my child.

You, always know this,
That I have made you a
Spiritual being
That sometimes
Resides in a human body,
And although this body

Juliet Christie Murray

Is slowed down,

Nothing can hold down
That powerful spirit that
I have entrusted to you,
Remember
You are
Very special to me,
And that's why, you.

I want you to know that
Where you are
Right now,
Is the place where
I God want you to be,
Make the most of it,
And keep on listening to me.

Do not think of yesterday,
Do not think of tomorrow,
Yesterday is gone
And I almighty God
Controls tomorrow.
I will always take care
Of you.
Because you
Are very, very,
Special to me.

December 21, 2002. Written especially for a 27 years old young lady with love, to help her get over the difficult times after she lost her leg in a motor vehicle accident.

Journey to Enlightenment

Rain Dance

I hear their soft feet dancing on the roof,
One, two, three, four, stamp, stamp, stamp.
It makes me also want to dance as
I listen to the beautiful music
Make by the raindrops dancing feet,

Loud music, soft music, light music,
Beating of the gullies drumming by,
Raindrops soft, light, sprinkling as they
Gloriously dance on pavement high
Out on this wonderful starless night.

Do you hear their dancing feet
Making music so sweet under the starless sky?
Do you dance with them in your heart
When you hear their soft, gentle, dancing feet?
Or do they send you gently off to sleep.
In the beautiful dreamy night.

May 2003. Jamaica is said to be a land of wood, water and rising hills. Nothing can be compared to a rainy night when one lives beside a gully course and hear the water fording off these hills.

Juliet Christie Murray

Lending A Helping Hand

I saw her standing there,
Torn between love and hate,
Torn for the child she bore.
Hate because her heart is sore,
For somehow she stands alone.

I saw her standing there,
Lost in bewilderment, confused,
For she knew not what to do,
For she was just too young
To know, too young to even care.

I saw her standing there,
Wondering, if someone will
Rescue a poor teenage mother
From the burden of ill,
Which is the destiny of rearing
This unborn child without a father.

I saw someone stopped to listen,
Someone with love and pity,
Who took hold of her hand
As she crosses
Life's raging stream.

Some one who
Knew the way,
Who had already
Passed that way,
For experience

Was her teacher.

February 12, 2003. Written after visiting a funeral of a 31-year-old mother who was murdered leaving five children, the first does not know his father. So many West Indian women are exposed to abuse, more so when they become teenage mothers without the assistance of the fathers.

Juliet Christie Murray

Achieving Your Dream

The road of life can be long
And seems so out of sight,
But if we try with all our might
We can obtain our dreams.

What is your dream?
To make it on the cricket team
That hit all or most of the balls
That forever comes on stream?

Do you dream of children grown
And many times around
Be part of their pleasant dream?
Or do we watch in sorrow since
Tomorrow for them is quite unknown?

The road of life we pleasantly try,
To do our very, very best.
In helping others who take a rest,
Too tired to live or strive.

Give of your best in all your quest,
For this is the only way,
In passing life's greatest test
And you'll surely achieve your dream.

February 11, 2003. Dreams are the eyes of the blind. Dreams give birth to realities.

Journey to Enlightenment

friend

He hurts me so.
Way down within my soul,
But I took no offence,
Because I know he is
Believed to be my friend.

He gave me so much,
More than any other did,
In times like these.
I am mighty pleased
To know he is my friend.

He shares my most inner thoughts.
I tell him all my wants,
Although sometimes he cannot supply.
He encourages me to try.
Because he is my friend.

When I am alone,
And in deep despair,
He is always there to cheer,
And I am very proud,
To know that he is my friend.

February 13, 2003. Friends should be forever. Friendship entails giving and receiving. Friends should help each other to grow.

Juliet Christie Murray

Three Steps Ahead

If you wish to climb 'successes ladder'
There must before you gather
These three rungs of the ladder
Good, better, best,
Forever, looming within your sight.

The rung of good is clearly seen,
The rung of better you strive to reach,
The rung of best keeps on shifting
Each time the feet aim higher.

For somewhere above you climb,
One for whom your best is only good,
So if for the top you strive,
Keep these three steps ahead
Continually within your sight.

If the top you do reach,
Where all the big lights streak,
Remember if there you will remain,
Always aim at these three steps ahead,
The steps of good, better, best.

September 2003. The inspiration for this poem came when I saw a sign for a
prep school 'Three Steps Ahead.'

Why Do I Cry

Why do I feel so sad?
I just want to cry,
In my room I sometimes go
Although I try not to do,
But I still break down and cry.

I am just thirteen
And have enough to eat,
I have lots of clothes
And many, many, friends
I should be happy!
Shouldn't I?

Am I too emotional?
Or am I bad?
I really don't think so,
Why then do I cry
When nothing seems wrong?

Mom says I am temperamental,
Teacher says it's my hormones,
Can someone tell me
Why do I cry
When nothing is really, really wrong?

February. 23, 2003. The inspiration came when I overheard a thirteen year old telling her friend that she cries and she does not know why. 'Oh the insecurity of youth.'

Juliet Christie Murray

Bridges

Let us build a bridge today,
It's an invitation for all
Who will accept this call,
For without it someone will fall
Because there is no easier way.

Why build a bridge?
It's built to aid those
Who know not life's un-chartered waters,
Those who are unable to swim,
Whose hearts are faint and frail.

It serves to convey
The messengers of hope,
From ages past
To the present
And to the future.

It will safely close the chasm
For those on the other side,
From what will we
Construct this bridge?
From material strong and inexpensive.

We will build it on,
The foundation of the almighty.
With steel of love,
Bricks of forgiveness,
Mortar of honesty,
Iron of integrity,

A strong bridge,
That anyone can trust.

Look out there on that bridge!
Some weary traveler is crossing,
Would he have made it?
That homeward journey,
If we hadn't stopped
To build that bridge?

March 2, 2003. Bridges are so important. Some of them are magnificent structures. They sometimes act as houses for destitute people, underneath them ships and water pass. On them trains, motor vehicle and individuals cross. They have to be strong; such should be life's bridges. Am I a bridge?

Juliet Christie Murray

The Fight

He left two nights before,
The girls came calling,
He returned sick unto death,
Poisoned,
So were the others.

He will not die!
He must not die!
I will not stand by and not try
Although from the doctor I stayed shy,
Surely he will not die.

Half bottle of expectorant.
Ten drops of iodine this night,
Tomorrow
Canadian Healing Oil,
You will not die.

Open your mouth and drink this milk,
Take these two spoons of tonic,
Swallow this water, salt and iodine,
Add to these some good lamp oil.

Why do you bother to try
When all his other friends have died?
From such poisoning there is no return,
Continue to medicate if you wish,
But he must prepare to die.

Ten days have past,

Journey to Enlightenment

And he hasn't taken a bite,
But faith, hope
And perseverance ignite
Oh! He has won this fight!

He lives!
He lives!
He lives at last!
My dog
Samba lives!

Written March 7,2003, when a number of dogs died from an insecticide poisoning in the community.

One made it through this ordeal, my dog, Simba with lots of love and will power. Dare to do the impossible. Dare to love enough.

Juliet Christie Murray

Jamaican Man

Hey you foreign gal,
Just go weh fran deh
Who want fi you foreign man?
Whole heap a man inna Jamaica,
An every gal can get har own a man,
Meck me tell you, we hav,

Beanie man
Elephant man
Ninja man
Yellow man
An nuff nuff
Maama man.

Jamaican man dem a the best
Any weh in a di east or west,
Them study fi pass every test,
An know how fi broke every country rule
Even if dem neva when go a school.

Jamaica man dem a di best,
Dem go a foreign fi go look money
Fi come back an gi dem honey,
But dem bring back nutten
Only whole heap a twanging.

Jamaican man a di best
Dem seh dem strong and
Hav whole heap a stamina,
So wha meck so much a dem

A teck 'Stamina RX'?

Hey! Jamaica man dem a try
Fi win di gold,
Fi father di biggest fold,
But me nah tell no lie
Dem really look like a fool.

When di pickney dem
A bawl an caan go a school,
For di mumma dem
Caan find no food.

Jamaica man a di best,
For dem can stand
Beside all di rest,
An when dem put on
Fi dem kine a big show,
The whole worl must know,
Dem a Jamaican man.

So gal go weh fran deh,
Just lef fi mi Jamaica man alone
For mi no want fi you foreign man,
As whole heap a man inna Jamaica
An every gal can get har own a man

For mi seh,
Jamaica man dem
A the best,
Of the best ,
Of the best !

October 9, 2003. The inspiration came when I heard two women quarreling for

Juliet Christie Murray

a man. Jamaican men stand tall among all the men in the world. They are very good at what they do, good or bad.

Children Of The King

Is your father the King?
Are you his children?
Do you hope to represent him
Some day?
All God's children are
Princes and princesses,
Because,
You are children of the king.

Let your thoughts and actions
Be kingly,
Your attire
Representing the king.
Robe your bodies in
Garments of light,
Integrity, discipline, and love,
For you are children of the king.

Out of you let your spirit soar,
Bringing with it ambition
To ignite that of the people
Who wait patiently on you
To show the way,
For you are
Children of the king.

Let your speech represent
Your father, the king
Let the words that escape your lips
Be those of encouragement and joy,

Juliet Christie Murray

Let them be like music of pure love,
Falling gentle on the ears of those
With whom you commune.

It's your legacy,
Bequeathed to you
By your father the king,
Grab it!
Take hold of it,
Use it well,
You are blessed.
You are children of the king.

April 2003. Written to let people realize that they are not on earth as mere human, but they are God's creation and are therefore special individuals with a purpose and should reflect good values and attitude.

The Pageant

The room is beautifully decorated,
Multi-coloured lights illuminate the stage,
The crowd sits
Eagerly,
Waiting,
Who will win the crown tonight?

Ordinary girls will vie for
The title of queen tonight,
Girls to whom before now
Most of the audience never
Even paused to say hello,
Now have this crowd of
Dignitaries and aristocrats quivering
On the edges of their seats,
All keyed up with hearts a beat.

The hour has come, and
All the introductions have been made,
Here they come all beautifully arrayed
In garments of purest white,
To display to the audience and judges
Their magnificent talents in dance.
Yes, they do their best to impress
As they pretend to be whom they are not.

Have they fooled us?
Of course they do; audience and judges alike,
For to this crowd and judges
They are all quite unknown,

Juliet Christie Murray

The die is cast.
One of the contestants has emerged,
She has won the crown,
And will triumphantly wear
Both sash and crown of Miss... 2003.

She will pretend for one whole year
To be an individual she is not,
But at the end of twelve months reign
She will have opened for her,
Knowledge
Dimensions,
Opportunities,
And horizons,
For here lies within her hands
Her destiny.

If the cards she does play well,
Then whatsoever hand,
She decides to deal,
This will be the beginning
Of the rest of her life.

Written May 2003, after attending a beauty pageant of a prominent hotel in Jamaica.

Jamaica has so many beautiful and talented people but many are never given the opportunity to show what they are capable of doing, only if it is profitable to those with the means to provide the openings.

Windows Of Life

There are many, many
Windows of life,
Picture windows
From which we look on
Different scenic views,
Some look on life's realities,
Pleasantness,
Such as
Love,
Beauty,
Health,
And wealth.
All beautifully etched
Within our windows' frames.

Some windows look out on
The reality of
unpleasantness,
Hatred,
War,
Mistrust,
And covetousness,
All prompted by
Un-forgiveness,
And unrequited love.
Oh sometimes we hang
Our heads in shame,
Because they are too depressing
To behold.

Juliet Christie Murray

Do we allow these drab scenes
To make us sad and depress,
Oh yes we do,
We can however change this,
By employing our
Imaginative powers
To create our own scenic views,
These we can gladly share,
With those whose
Realities are blank walls.

For such, we may be coveted,
And may be pushed aside,
But oh what a disappointment,
For he who instigated the move,
To find when he has gotten
Our window,
Only to discover he is,
Looking out just,
On a plain blank wall.

May 23 2003. The mind is a very powerful instrument and can be utilized to create whatever one wishes to see. It is not good to covet any one's possession or position. The grass always looks greener on the other side. Love, justice and courage are the keys to your window.

Journey to Enlightenment

Twenty One Years

For twenty one years
I've loved you so,
Though chained for
These past twenty-five,
Many tears I've wept and dried
As life seem so unfair and unkind,
Yet I am so glad I've loved
And have been loved by you.

Sometimes life gets so depressing,
And almost unbearable when
The people who should care,
Seem so uncaring and so unkind,
But thoughts of you illuminate the way
And give me the strength to go on.

Sometimes I try to soar above,
The things that get me down,
Unpleasantness, life, and individuals,
Just when I feel as though I will fall
Feelings of you come rushing by,
And you become the wind beneath my wings.

For these twenty-one years you have
Remain a constant image etched within my mind,
And most of what I do and say, I do,
Believing that somehow your spirit lingers near,
And is really proud of me.

For ten years I've conjure up images of you,

Juliet Christie Murray

Are you fat, are you old, are you gray,
But somehow I could not change the images
Of your love and your kindness that are
Already engraved within my mind.

And then I saw you after ten long years,
And realize that you certainly have changed.
Your hair have become gray,
And in some places silvery white,
And the struggles of life have
Deepened the lines within your face.

But I noticed something most incredible.
You have matured as I have matured,
Both physical and spiritual, and
Our love had matured into a love,
That will be sustained no matter where we are.

We both realize that to sustain such a love,
Is to take care of the individuals to whom
We are bounded to by integrity and promise,
For true love, as the master said
Is
In as much as you have done it unto others
You have done it unto me.

Just a glimpse or a call from you
Once in a long while.
That's all I'll ever need.
To keep on updating.
My physical images of you.
For though sometimes I feel so
Alone and so unloved,
Just that one look or call from you

Journey to Enlightenment

Will make life seem worthwhile,
For my emotional memories of you
Will surely never ever die.

June 14, 2003. True love and kindness never dies. True love allows one to wish
the best for the other. True love always want the other person to be happy, no
matter what it takes.

Juliet Christie Murray

I'm Crying Today

I am crying today
For failed expectations.
I am crying today
For I am
Bounded
By duty
And integrity
And promise.

I am crying today
For I am feeling so alone,
No one knows that I cry
Only you
Because
I'm sure you are crying too.

My heart cries most of the times
As I go about my daily duties,
I smile and speak pleasant words
But no one but you really knows
How my heart really cries.

My heart cries today
For I am longing for
A fleeting glimpse of you
That will remind me that
Though we are far apart,
A glance will reaffirm
We are still friends
That's why my heart cries.

Journey to Enlightenment

When will these hearts stop crying?
When you are gone
Or when I am gone?
Never!
They will cry more as there will be
That constant numb, dull, ache.
For you can never be replaced.

Oh if these two hearts were free,
Free from the chains of integrity,
Then maybe we'd be free to,
Talk
Laugh
Sing
And dance as before,
Then my tears will be dry
And my heart would sing again,
As I'm sure yours would too,
Oh how I miss you so.

June 14, 2003. A lament for a lost friendship of a very close friend, because of the unkindness and injustice of a life partner.

Juliet Christie Murray

Evening Of Praise

The stage is set,
The cameras are all rolling,
The choir takes the center stage,
The great, powerful, mighty, God,
The supreme, creator of the universe
Is petitioned to take up his abode,
For praises, will be rendered
To him this evening.

Great God of wonder
God of Light,
Listen a while
As your people
Render to you,
Their accolades
Of praises
In songs.

Oh mighty God of grace.
Who gave these talents to these people
Here now showing
Love and adoration,
As they peal out notes
In voices clear and pure,
As tears stream down their faces
In sheer joy and adulation.

The songs they sing, echo,
Messages of faith and hope
Which are grounded in you.

Journey to Enlightenment

'Shout to the Lord'
'On time God',
'Roll you over the tide'
'When Jesus comes'.

Great omnipresent God,
You should be proud indeed,
And hope that these
Your people unspoken wish,
Be,
That you will ever,
Keep them singing your praise.

Hold them
Very close Lord,
That they won't miss
Your heart beat.
And don't let them ever
Wander away.

June 2002 written at the evening of praise concert held at Montego Bay S.D.A
Conference.

Juliet Christie Murray

Farewell

Squish, squash,
Squish squash,
Now the sea raises its head and flicks its tail,
Beating its foaming mane,
Dashing it so methodically on
White sand beaches and jagged rocks.

Here on this jetty I sit,
Watching and waiting
For the sea to churn and spray
Its salty waters in cascades all over me,
My heart lifts
My soul opens and explodes
As my sprit soars.

The cold November morn chills my bones
With its clean, crisp freshness,
As the gentle morning breeze
Whispers among the trees and within my hair,
This is the most beautiful time of the year
When sea and wind celebrate the gentle
Creeping in of winter.

The birds render their last symphony
A goodbye to the departing fall,
It's the time when I escape from my childhood
Duties to meet with them
And have lots of fun on the quays,
Skipping the waves as the wind
Lifts my skirt high as a kite

Journey to Enlightenment

Flying over the foaming waves,
While I bid a last farewell
To my friend John twit.

Feb 12, 2004, just sitting on the beach one afternoon reminiscing on my childhood days by the sea on the beautiful sunny Caribbean island of Jamaica.

Juliet Christie Murray

Sunshine And Rain

Hey!
Here they are,
They are best of friends,
They are dancing to
The same music of
God's great
And marvelous creation.

They are
Neither feeling
Hot nor cold,
They are supportive
Of each other,
In the same
Time and space.

They are bringing us a message,
Message of unity and cooperation,
They teach us humans
That we can be best of friends
Though our ideas differ.

Oh!
They are indeed,
Exhilarating to behold!
As they entwine,
They form the most beautiful,
Of rainbow colours.

Yes!

Journey to Enlightenment

The raindrops and the
Beautiful sunshine are happy,
None is trying to outdo the other
You see they are best of friends today.

June 22 2003. Written after seeing the sun shining with all its strength during a heavy shower of rain.

Juliet Christie Murray

Debil An Him Wife

But tap,
A seh cooyah,
Oonoo see me dying trial yah,
Oonoo see wha me a see?
In yah this yah broad middle day,
Debil an him wife a fight?

Wha you seh ooman?
Seh you neva hear seh
Debil hav wife?
You neva hear bout her?
So, a weh you come from?
You no live inna J.A.?

But oonoo look yah
Now though eenee.
Ooman,
You no see seh the rain
And the sun a put aann
A juice of a fight?

The two a dem a try fi
See a who a wear the trousez.
Hey!
Hey!
Hey!
Dem a try fi out do each other,
But none a dem nah win,
For a long time,
The two a dem a galang

Out deli same way,

June 23, 2003. A Jamaican concept of the implication of what it means when the sun and the rain are occupying the same time and space. 'Men and women trying to dominate each other'.

Juliet Christie Murray

Examination Time

1st Per.

"Whoa mi deh go mad!"

2nd Per.

"If I die, it will have been from a heart attack brought on by the marking of examination papers."

3rd Per.

"Jesus, Mi, want a nedda jab".

4th Per.

"Boy, mi just caan teach again,"

2ndPer.

"What are we going to do with these children?

I can't even read what they write!

I tell you,

Did you know that factory can be spelt as?

F. A. C. H .R, I,?"

3rd Per.

"Yes mi dear.

Misses queen would a tan inna inglan

An drop down stiff dead,

Fi see how the new technological age,

Decide fi change up her English wud dem."

"Cause, how she wen learn fi spell dem

A no so dem spell again."

1st Per.

"Wah wrong wid fi wi education system in a Jamaica though eene?"

Pinckney come from grade one straight to grade nine, an caan even spell him own a name?"

4th Per.

Mi a tell you seh,

Journey to Enlightenment

Sometime me proud fi be a teacher,
But right yah now chile,
As mi a mark dem yah 2003,
Examination papa,
Mi no proud mi a teacher at all.
Student.
Take heart dear teach,
For if you did eva know,
The whole heap a teacher,
Wha teach me,
An how much wok
Mi did ha fi put eene,
So,
That mi can write F.A. C .H .R. I,
That you can know a wah,
Just with a little more wok
From you, and mi, alike,
Then,
One day,
Mi know,
Mi wi get it right."

July 2003. The inspiration came from marking end of year examination papers, and found I had to decode a number of the sentences the students wrote. The other side of the coin is, many children are really trying very hard to learn to read and write. What may seem, as failure to some is sometimes great achievement for others.

Juliet Christie Murray

Where Are The dogs

What a mix,
This city with people and traffic
But where are the dogs?
Are there none in Brooklyn
To walk the streets of this city?

Oh they are here indeed,
But these are precious,
Little creatures,
That deserves protection,
And to be treated kindly indeed.

They are too important to be
Allowed to walk the streets of the city,
This is a privilege reserved for,
The poor,
The not so ambitious,
The homeless, and the blacks.

Brooklyn,
This place, of stark duality,
So many opportunities opened,
To all who dare to seize,
Food galore for the poor,
From people with over flowing stores.

A sure place for third world blacks to be,
As they are seen as deserving to
Remain with their kind,
Since birds of a feather,

Should flock together,
Because they are more easily defined.

Yes the once mighty Brooklyn streets
Now belong almost exclusive,
To the blacks.
Whites and dogs are
Too important to be there.

August 2003. A perspective on Brooklyn after driving through this part of New York City and saw that most of the people were blacks. Many parts of that area were so dilapidated .I saw no dogs walking the streets as seen in most Caribbean islands.

Juliet Christie Murray

New York

New York City you stand there
Tall and sprawling,
Believing that you are invincible
And will last forever.

For embedded within your bowels
Are the offspring of all
Nations
Tongues
And people.

Found here within your borders,
Are the consistent rise
And fall of heart beats,
The persistent humming of traffic
As they honk and toot their horns,
Under the sleepless eyes of street lights,
Cameras, police and street people.

New York City
You who mothered most,
You, who have nurtured,
Both the weak and strong,
You are the pot that boils
And the cast that mold
Those within your borders,
Willing or unwilling to be shaped,

Whoever or whatever they have become,
Great or small,

Journey to Enlightenment

You were instrumental in their making,
Don't turn them away now,
Continue to nurture them.

Because, without them you are nothing,
Without them you are lost and doomed,
Because these are the ones
Who make you great.

July 2003. Written after spending a few days in New York City and observed
the many categories of people especially in down town Manhattan which give
this city life and its unique flair.

Juliet Christie Murray

The Uncles

You gave me my first ballpoint pen.
You gave it with all your heart
And without reservation,
Some may say it's only a ballpoint pen,
But to me, in the year 1960,
It was like a diamond set in gold,
For then, in Jamaica
It was a rare novelty.

But, that was not the most important thing
You gave me a love beyond compare,
The love that a child needed
From a mother and a father
Absent and unknown,
No one can ever understand
Not even you for sure,
How much you had really done for me.

You let me feel that I was somebody,
Where, before I was not quite so sure.
You allowed me to be a child
Free and uninhibited,
I could ask you the most foolish questions
A child could ever ask,
I could throw the biggest tantrum
A child would dare to throw.

When I was through, your love was
Very much the same.
A wonderful feeling, that truly was.

Journey to Enlightenment

You gave me a lot,
To some it may seem so little,
But to me it was so very much
Because it was given from the heart.
A heart that many believe you do not possess.

You see there was a connection
No one will comprehend,
As the longing to know a mother
Who is very much alive
Creates an ache that only you and I
Will ever understand,
We are kindred spirits
Created almost alike.

That's what emotional starvation
Renders unto people just like us.
We are products of struggle
Determination and ambition,
Individuals who make the best of
Situations though tricky they seem,
People who work to create
Whom and what we are.

You need to know
That though I am now fifty-two
Showing me New York City today,
I felt like a little child again,
I could still ask you the simplest of questions,
Others would think me foolish to ask.
I still had that same faith in you,
Just like when I was a child.

If at this time in your life,
Juliet Christie Murray

You are plagued by
How others may see you
Good, bad, or unkind,
You be very certain that, to me
There is no other person in the world like you,
For without you, I would still not know
Exactly who I am.

You have helped me to find my roots,
For this I am very, very glad,
If other abandoned, homeless, hopeless children,
Had an uncle just like you,
Who entered their lives
At strategic times like mine,
This world would surely be
A better place for humans
To live and to die.

I love you,
I salute you
And all other uncles,
Just like you.

August 2003. Written and dedicated to my uncle Marcus Davis who has always treated me so, special, even when I was a little girl.

Haughty Fought

Is your life a good fight?
Or is it indeed a haughty fought?
For never ever should we
Let the slip of the tongue,
Cause us to confuse these words.
You see it is deemed indeed,
That out of the abundance of the heart,
The mouth speaks.

At times we fool ourselves,
That we are fighting a great fight,
We launch our own cannons,
And blow our own trumpets,
While other soldiers see us,
As just fighting a haughty 'fought'.
Because we are self centered
Pumped up with our own importance

We pretend to live exemplary lives,
When the true aim is to show,
Others their own inadequacies.
At the end of our task,
It is very disappointing
When others try to laud us
But, by a slip of the tongue states
We have fought a haughty fought,
Instead of a haughty fight.

For out of the abundance
Of the heart,

Juliet Christie Murray

The mouth does
Speak

September 25 2003. Written after hearing a tribute at a funeral service where the speaker by the slip of his tongue used the incorrect tense of the word fight in his closing sentence that completely changed the meaning of pages and pages of accolades. To Jamaicans the sound of the word fought could mean (fart, phartz), air, gasbag, emptiness.

Train the Child

Life is a struggle
When you try to juggle,
The meager resources
Against the bill forces.

People are crying
Because things are rough,
But to tell you the truth
Life is really, really, tough.

Now the children are crying
For the food is not enough,
It seem all are gone to the dogs
As the economy supports only the big boys.

While the small boys learn
To loot and shoot,
Rape and maim and some will kill
To pay the children's school bills.

The governments baffle
For they know not how to tackle,
The problem of the poor
Who come crying at their door

Every week we receive a package
Of deportees who bring the wreckage,
The big countries seem weak,
And cannot control these freaks.

Juliet Christie Murray

Jamaica is now in worries
As ever day she buries,
Those slain by the gun
This is really, really no kind of fun.

Train up the child in the way he should go,
This may stop him from growing wild,
And relieve the pain upon our brows,
For he may grow into a perfect child.

September 28, 2003. Jamaica is riddled with crime. This has escalated with the return of criminals from the U.S.A. They have brought with them more sophisticated methods of criminality, which has proven to be more cruel and wicked than that of the locals.

All Is Not Lost

"Teacher please,
May I borrow
A needle and thread"?
This was a request
From a strong, robust
Fourteen year old boy,
A student of grade nine.

"What do you need those for"?
The teacher asked.
"To sew a girl's uniform
That I tore,"
He said.

Fifteen minutes later
There he was sitting
With the needle and
Thread in his hand,
And the girl's
Uniform in his lap
Sewing away merrily.

There came the
Home economics teacher,
"Son," she said,
"It was good I taught you to sew,"
"Yes teacher."
He said.

"Me too,"

Juliet Christie Murray

Said another,
Standing close by,
"I'm glad you
Taught me to sew,
I sew my shirt this morning".

With hands clasp
As if in prayer
And with head bowed in
Reverence and respect
He said
"Thank you teacher
For teaching me to sew".

September 28, 2003. As teachers it seem as though our work is in vain especially when we are blamed for students not performing well in national examinations. All is not lost. When we can be thanked for the little things that students appreciate; things that will never be reflected on examination papers, not measurable, we have taught. Keep on doing the good work teachers.

Journey to Enlightenment

Alone is Better

The dogs are barking,
The telephones are ringing,
The television is blaring,
A friend comes calling,
Am I lonely ?
No
But I am alone.

Here I sit night after night
In this big four bedroom house,
The envy of so many women,
Am I lonely?
No,
But I am alone.

I watch the television,
I write,
I sew
I read three different books at once,
I eat all I dare to eat,
I wonder, do I eat too much,
I look in the mirror and ask myself
Am I getting too fat?
Will I get sick?

I shouldn't ask,
At this present moment I am sick,
Sick of sitting here night after night,
This was not what I bargained for
Am I lonely?

Juliet Christie Murray

No,
I am just alone.

Where is the man I married
So that I wouldn't be alone?
It's now eleven p. m., where is he?
Last night he came home at nine,
He was here I was not alone,
But oh God I was so lonely.

You see
I could not read him,
I could not hear him,
I barely saw him,
I knew not what to say to him
We were like strangers,
Heck alone is better,

Written Nov. 2003. This a typical experience of many West Indian women
whose men stay out late at nights. Some children hardly know their dad although
he lives at home. Some men have more than one family.

Journey to Enlightenment

The Revelation

Water is pouring from all over me,
Creating a river,
That flows in and out of
The depths of my soul,
I can't control it,
I must let it flow.
This flood of Inspiration,
Pouring forth out of me.

There is this energy gushing
From deep within me,
This energy that seeks to ignite,
All who dear to come near,
It whispers to me saying
Others are,
Your sisters, your brothers,
Your sons, your daughters,
Love them in all the ways you can.

Let them all know they are
Children of that great Universal Spirit,
Individuals with the potential, to dig deep
Within the bowels of their souls,
And unearth that Great Spirit
Who will enable them
To be the best there is
Of what they can ever be.

Get up harness that universal spirit,
Buried every where, and in every one,

Juliet Christie Murray

I have found it, and has allowed
This universal Holy Spirit
To dwell and have free reign in me.
He has, and is about to do,
Such marvelous things in me,
If I just allow him to have,
His own free way in me.

Water is flowing all over me,
A peace that comes from deep within,
I have made peace with my perfections,
And with my imperfections,
I now take up this mission,
To do my part in whatever I can,
In helping to heal this sad, sick world,
Full of Gods wonderful, beautiful people,
The crowning glory of his creation.

I now make this my creed,
'I love every one and
Hope every one loves me'.
And I must accept that each
Will show it in ways
Good , bad or unkind,
His own unique way.

Written October 15, 2003. This is the last piece in this book 'Journeys To
Enlightenment', a revelation piece.

Journey to Enlightenment

Glossary

Some of the pieces in this book are written in Jamaican dialect.

Although there is no hard and fast rule to the interpretation to the Jamaican dialect, below are some of the meanings for some of the dialect used in this book.

The Jamaican dialect differs in parishes and among the social classes of the Jamaican people.

Aan	on
Blud	blood
Caan	cannot can
Cooya	look here
Debil	devil
Dan	than
Dat	that
Dem	they them
Deh	there
Dem deh	those
Fah	for
Fi	to
Fi mi	mine
Gi weh	give away
Fran	from
Gal	girl
Galang	go on
Gi	give
Hav	have
Har	her
Maama man	a sissy
Meck	make
Mi	me, I

Juliet Christie Murray

Mumma	mother
Neda	another
Neva	never
Nutten	nothing
Nuff	plenty
Oofa	whose
Ooman	woman
Pan	on
Pickney	children
Tan	stay
Tan up	stand
Teck	take
Wah	what
Weh	where
Wud	word
Worl	world
Yah	here

Index Of Themes

Juliet Christie Murray

Journey to Enlightenment

Biography

Juliet Christie Murray (Soy Criada) was born 1950 in the quiet little district of Roslyn in the parish of Hanover on the beautiful Caribbean island of Jamaica. She spent her first five years living with her grandmother. Later she lived with her grand uncle until she was nineteen years old when she decided to go and live on her own. Her life has been one of struggle and determination. All this has created the foundation for all her accomplishments. She attended the Lucea Primary School where she also started her teaching career 1970 as a pupil teacher. She later went on to study at the Caenwood Junior Teacher's College in 1972 and received a junior teacher certificate. In 1977 she received her teacher's certificate in primary education from the Ministry of Education.

In 1988 she received her teacher's diploma in (Home Economics) technical education in which she majored in nutrition from the College of Arts Science and Technology.

In 2003 she received her bachelor's degree in sociology and applied social relations from Eastern Connecticut State University U.S.A.

She is married and is the mother of two boys. She has interest in alternative medicine and holds certificates in Swedish massage, Reflexology and Sports Injury massage.

She also has interest in interior decorating and holds a certificate in interior decorating. She holds other certificates in leadership and computer technology.

Juliet began writing poetry in June 2002. She completed the major part of the manuscript for this, her first book in 2003 and started presenting her pieces to live audiences that same year. In March 2004 she performed at the World Poetry Day Festival held in Kingston Jamaica. Later in that same month one of her pieces was recorded live for the CPTC Television programme. Lyrically

Speaking, hosted by Mutabaruka. Two of her pieces were used as speech entries In the Jamaica Festival Of Arts speech Competition 2004. In May 2004 she did live presentation at the Calabash International Literary Festival Jamaica.

Juliet is a practicing Home Economics teacher and is also a Vice Principal at the Sandy Bay Primary and Junior high school in Hanover, Jamaica. She is a member of Kiwanis International.

Notes and Comments

Journey to Enlightenment

ISBN 1412036232

9 781412 036238